Abiding Love

Sacred Thoughts and Verses
BY AUDREY McDANIEL

Floral Designs
BY HAZEL HOFFMAN

Published by
THE C. R. GIBSON COMPANY

In memory of RENAH BLAIR RIETZKE, an
inspired life whose magnificent
contribution in the cause of hope
reflected . . . The Abiding Love of Jesus.

Copyright © MCMLXXIII by
The C. R. Gibson Company, Norwalk, Connecticut
All rights reserved
Printed in the United States of America
Library of Congress Catalog Card Number: 73-78371
ISBN: 0-8378-1734-X

THE ONE ROSE

A perfect Rose grew on the earth
In days of long ago
It had a special mission
As you and I both know
It came to earth a tiny Bud
With petals to unfold
That as they opened we might see
Fine jasper and rare gold
Its perfume gave a fragrance rare
Which souls may also do
If we will turn to God above
And to our Lord be true
Then as this Rose had opened wide
Its very heart to see
One knew this was the beauty
God sought in you and me
Then as its blooming ended
In quiet and sweet repose
God planned a further mission
For this One precious Rose
That in this world for you and me
One Rose would bloom eternally.

Jesus came to confirm in the
earth . . . the precious Promises
of God.

*   *   *

And they shall be my people,
and I will be their God:

And I will give them one heart,
and one way . . .

And I will make an everlasting
covenant with them, that I will
not turn away from them, to do
them good . . .

Yea, I will rejoice over them
to do them good, and I will
plant them in this land
assuredly with my whole heart
and with my whole soul.

Jeremiah 32:38-41

O ROSE
OF THE GARDEN

When things of life shall
    fail you
And hope shall disappear
Remember God's one precious Rose
Will be forever near
All needs shall then be answered
Through Christ, the Gift of Love
From God our heavenly Father
O thank Thee Lord above.

All too often our brother's
path is so filled with care
he is blinded in the matter
of faith.

But Jesus taught us that His
Father has provided help for
all of the needs of mankind.

He can use others who are in
a position to look objectively
at the situations of those in
need . . . and as we pray in faith
and loving concern . . . God takes
over.

BECAUSE
IN FAITH

O Lord for others let us pray
Dear Father use our lives each day
To bear the pain and suffering too
The heartbreak that our Saviour knew
Till clouds and burdens disappear
Because in faith we bring Thee near
The healing Love of Christ impart
Dear Father hear us from the heart.

How often when burdened and in
deep despair has Jesus stayed
close by.

Faithfully sheltering us from
the storms of life that beset
us.

Then as the clouds are lifted
through His patient, tender
Love . . . would that we put our
hand in His with a total
commitment.

Master, O faithful Love—
I'll go with you all the way!

Yes, I want to talk to you Lord
Of the things that trouble me
For I know that in your mercy
You can set my sad heart free
I should like to tell you Master
Of my grievances and shame
For I know your great compassion
Can redeem my soul from blame
I'd bare my hopes and
        dreams dear Lord
For your blessing and your grace
With my hand in yours my Saviour
Close beside you face to face.

Once we have come to an
awareness of Jesus' perfect
Love and His Spirit has
permeated our being — we then
long to be freed of self and
become one in purpose with
Him.

It is then we seek to share
this fulfilling experience
with others as expressed in
the immortal words of Jesus.

       * * *

. . . Holy Father, keep through
thine own name those whom
thou hast given me, that they
may be one, as we are.

John 17:11

TRULY ONE

As Christ lingered there
    beside me
With His comfort and His Love
I knew He was the dearest Gift
That came from heaven above
I bid Him tarry with me
Wished that He would never go
For my heart at last was happy
In this rare and sacred glow
All at once 'twas plain before me
And I knew the reason why
For the beauty of His Spirit
Filled all space of earth and sky
I believed in God the Father
And in Jesus Christ His Son
For the Love that filled these
    moments
Made us really, truly one.

Quietly . . . in majestic splendor
God lights His little heavenly
lamps — the tiny stars — in the
still of night.

To give us sweet repose and
illuminate our path below.

Likewise does His canopy of
Love enfold us every waking
moment.

Tender wings of security and
peace that cover our every
need.

            *   *   *

. . . the earth is full of thy
riches.

Psalm 104:24

O then my dear Father . . .
As I gently pray . . . Send
my heart on a song . . . And
in service away.

Lord, give me serious things
to do . . . Things that hold
meaning just for You . . . Cause
me to ponder thoughts divine . . .
To please Thee, Lord, for I
am Thine . . . Lead me to those
in need of prayer . . . Help me
to show them Thou dost care.

　　　*　*　*

Bless ye the Lord, all ye his
hosts; ye ministers of his,
that do his pleasure.

　　　　Psalm 103:21

INSTRUMENTS
FOR GOD

In your vineyard God I'd tarry
As an instrument of Thine
And I'd pray to heaven above me
That my life with love would shine
Ever seeking Lord to comfort
Those grown faint and weary too
Offering them a cup of water
As my Saviour bid me do
Use my life O precious Father
Let my Saviour lead the way
From the hours of the morning
Till at night I kneel to pray
Storing treasures up in heaven
Fruits of sacred deeds well done
Till I hear my Master saying
Child of God, we now are one.

Would that Jesus' Way of Love
permeate our very souls . . .
that in the faith of a little
child . . . we may come to know
His Way as one of simple
truth.

His divine ministry was based
on two things . . . to love . . . and
to believe.

For love believeth all things . . .
hopeth all things . . . endureth
all things . . . love never ends.

And love is rooted in faith,
through confidence in God.

Would that we come to accept
with our minds the things
we can understand and all other
things through faith in God.

SIMPLICITY

And though in wisdom
   I shall grow
And many worthwhile
   things shall know
No matter what my
   learning be
Lord, make a trusting
   child of me.

The first day of the week cometh
Mary Magdalene early, when it was
yet dark, unto the sepulchre, and
seeth the stone taken away from
the sepulchre.

Jesus saith unto her, Mary. She
turned herself, and saith unto
him, Rabboni; which is to say,
Master.

John 20:1, 16

*   *   *

If only our hearts would draw
nigh unto Jesus in devotion as
Mary did . . . we could then feel
the sacred impact of the true
garden experience.

Jesus had befriended Mary and
her life without Him was
meaningless.

But Jesus understood how sorely
she did grieve after Him and
appeared to her the very first . . .
So will He befriend all those
who turn to Him.

THE
EASTER
LOVE

I want to walk with Jesus
  every step of the way
To have His goodness sanctify
  each word I say
To follow Him through valley
To the mountains high above
Down every path, through
  every garden
To offer Him my love
To be like Mary Magdalene
Who walked with Him one day
Who felt such pain and anguish
When they took her Lord away
That Love so real appeared to her
When He her name did say
Then Mary found her peace of soul
When Christ stood there that day
He was her one true love you see
Like Mary may He walk with me.

The Peace of Meditation—

O Father, we treasure the moments
when we may stand before Thee in
deep silence.

In this atmosphere of serenity
and love . . . we shall come to
know that thy blessings are
resting upon us . . . and that
these diamond seconds are
filled with Thy Grace.

* * *

. . . and in this place will I give
peace, saith the Lord of hosts.

Haggai 2:9

PEACE
SUPREME

Dear Father teach me this to know
In stress of life with hope dimmed low
That Thou canst weave a peace supreme
That is so real and not a dream
If in Thy arms we place each care
And understand that Thou art there
Then when our hearts with peace shall flow
To know our Father willed it so
Our anxious hearts to rest in Thee
Thou art our help eternally.

How can I get to God?

This is a question so often
asked by those who are
manifesting a tendency to
lean on self.

But man cannot run the course
of his life, try as he may.

He must lean on the power of
God to do all things.

It is as simple as this . . . when
we yield and meditate on what
He is . . . and forget self . . . so
that only His perfection
surrounds us . . . all things
take shape and form.

We then find ourselves not
struggling to get to God.

For in the reassurance and
quiet calm we feel — we are
actually in His very midst
drawn there by His patient,
tender Love.

O Father when that little me
Is cast so far I cannot see
Not even my own guilt and shame
But thy perfection can proclaim
My spirit soars to heights anew
I long O God to be like you
And when a change is wrought
        in me
My soul has met the heart of Thee.

I say confess. . .

The force of yesterday's
mistakes need not become an
instrument of destruction.

For if we confess to God that
we are in perfect agreement with
His judgment of us . . . and we do
truly repent . . . we shall then feel
the peace of His forgiveness
coming through.

Jesus taught us that no man has
the right to judge us . . . nor do
we have the right to judge others.

Only our Father who is perfect Love
has the right to condemn but
He will forever take us back to
His great heart . . . promising to
remember our evil no more.

Thus we are not working for the
approval of man but of God.

And when my evils plagued
      me
Regrets my sad heart filled
The words of my dear Jesus
My weary soul then stilled
With mercy and redemption
God takes thee to His breast
O Lord through such forgiveness
I know my life is blest.

Tenderly . . . in the infinite
meadows of creation blossom
the flowers of the angels . . .
FRIENDS.

These priceless jewels give
a sacred sparkle to our
existence.

May we ever preserve the
true meaning of Friendship . . .
a constant love . . . and
unselfish concern.

For the immortal conversation
of Jesus with His disciples
laid the foundation for
Friendship . . . "And I give an
example of love unto you . . .
that ye do unto others as I
have done unto you."

*   *   *

And they shall be mine, saith
the Lord of hosts, in that day
when I make up my jewels . . .

Malachi 3:17

26

Did a struggling, longing
brother
Come into my midst today
And though he didn't speak
a word
Was he asking me to pray
Did he have the need of
Friendship
Or a problem tugging there
And did I fail to take the
time
To lift him up in prayer
For Jesus bid the extra
mile
We walk with friends each day
No matter what the hour
or need
To turn them not away.

Let not your heart be troubled . . .

Jesus spent His entire ministry
trying to ease the heartbreak of
mankind . . . assuring us that in
every nook and crevice His Father
had placed symbols of hope.

Beyond the cloud . . . a rainbow.
For every tear . . . a smile.

No matter what the problem . . .
Jesus taught us that . . .
Faith in God the Father and in
Him . . . would give us a peaceful
solution to all things.

For faith leads to the secret place
of the Almighty, where in the arms
of His Love . . . we may find the
rainbow's end . . . contentment.

* * *

When my soul fainted . . . I remembered
the Lord . . .

Jonah 2:7

28

O Jesus how I treasure
Your perfect Love divine
To know that from my God
    above
This Love is really mine
Thy dear, sweet calm
    my soul doth fill
I know . . . Thy peace my
    fears can still.

Just as the still of winter
tucks the flowers to sleep . . .
so shall faith and hope . . . lie
dormant in our hearts at
times.

But just as God causes a tiny
crocus to herald the beautiful
resurrection and the majesty
of springtime . . . so shall His
saving Grace cause . . . faith
and hope . . . to blossom anew in
our lives.

God touched each tiny
    sleeping flower
And all at once a
    precious bower
Sprang forth in hope and
    faith anew
As symbols of His Love
    for you
A fragrance now so sweet
    and rare
Caused silent hearts this
    joy to share
As quiet winter passed
    away
These precious flowers
    seemed to say
We thank Thee, Lord, for
    Thy dear keep
But most of all to wake
    from sleep.

God's plan of creation is
perfect for He enhanced
the garden of life with
the gift of a dear
Saviour . . . who is perfect
Love.

Then He added friendships,
bird songs and sonnets.

We need never search for
love . . . for Jesus is ever
with us . . . nor will He ever
withhold His Love from us.

He is ever beseeching us to
find our security in His
eternal promise.

* * *

. . . and, lo, I am with you alway,
even unto the end of the world.

Matthew 28:20

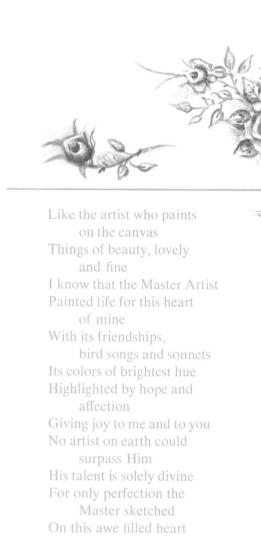

Like the artist who paints
    on the canvas
Things of beauty, lovely
    and fine
I know that the Master Artist
Painted life for this heart
    of mine
With its friendships,
    bird songs and sonnets
Its colors of brightest hue
Highlighted by hope and
    affection
Giving joy to me and to you
No artist on earth could
    surpass Him
His talent is solely divine
For only perfection the
    Master sketched
On this awe filled heart
    of mine.

Then Jesus saith unto them,
Children, have ye any meat?
They answered him, No.

And he said unto them, Cast
the net on the right side
of the ship, and ye shall
find.

John 21:5-6

* * *

So it is to this day . . . Jesus
is asking, doth any man have
lack.

If so, cast your net . . .
in faith . . . on the right
side of the ship where He is
standing . . . as a reminder that
God is our source of supply
with a grace sufficient for
our every need.

Thank God that Jesus
left the word
That through the ages
will be heard
There's grace sufficient
when we pray
His words will never
pass away.

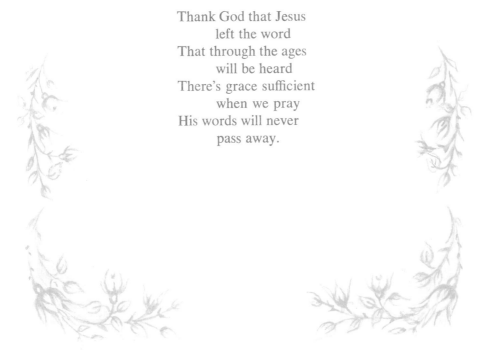

Even in the creation of a
tiny bird we see the
Master's Hand . . . and glimpse
direction.

With serenity and security
the little bird sings its
cheery song for God is its
Keeper.

This brings to mind the
words of Peter when He
said to Jesus . . . "Where
would I go Lord if it were
not to Thee, for Thou hast
the words of eternal life."

SERENITY

A bird sang forth with all his might
As setting sun foretold the night.
I, too, felt peace within
     my heart
The tiny bird this did impart
His cloak was warm, his eyes
     were bright
And beauty filled this heavenly
     sight
In God he sought his only keep
For waking hours or hours of
     sleep
White dogwood blossoms framed
     the scene
He sat there sheltered so serene
He had a Father up above
Who cared for him with tenderest
     Love
Which taught me 'twas to God
     to go
For like the bird He loved me so.

Thanks be to God He ordained
that life should be like a
beautiful . . . Amen.

Let it be so . . . for among
His constant and unfailing blessings we
find Faith . . . Hope . . . and Love.

FAITH . . . the belief and confidence
     in God for things both
     seen and unseen.

HOPE . . . expectancy of fulfillment
     through trust in God.

LOVE . . . the unselfish concern for
     others . . . that accepts them
     as they are with devotion
     and affection.

Dusk with soft shadows falling
At the quiet close of day
Moments of meditation
When I turn to God to pray
There in the evening silence
I ask my Father above
Please hear my earnest pleading
Watch o'er Thy people with love
Strengthen their faith dear Father
Bless them each step of the way
Then grant them peace in sleep Lord
Thy sweet Amen of the day.

A ROSE is pressed
between each line
The Love of Christ
complete, divine.